My City
is a
Murder of Crows

My City
is a
Murder of Crows

NIKITA PARIK

Hawakal
PUBLISHERS

New Delhi | Calcutta

HAWAKAL PUBLISHERS
70 B/9 Amritpuri, East of Kailash, New Delhi 65
33/1/2 K B Sarani, Mall Road, Calcutta 80

Email info@hawakal.com
Website www.hawakal.com

Cover designed by Bitan Chakraborty

First edition (paperback) July 2022

ISBN: 978-93-91431-42-6 (paperback)

Price: INR 350 | USD 14.99

For Mom and *Dad,* the wind beneath my wings
For Khushi and *Vibhu,* tiny wonders of my world

To God, for sustaining me in the dark times

Introduction

This collection has four distinct chapters. So the book becomes the body, and you begin with its heart—the heart of the city: the cities we live in, the cities we travel to, the towns we dance in and out of—physically, emotionally, through pixels on a screen, through roots and wings. From the heart, you move up to the mouth—a scripture, an ocean, a city, sometimes a prayer, a script, a lonely urbanscape. From the mouth, you dive deep into the pit of the abdomen—a cavity that witnesses all our heartbreaks and disappointments; a sinking ship, a dementia of breathing. Finally, from the abdomen, the feverish words disperse through the rest of the body by electric nerve channels. Here, you discover poems on Covid, poems written post-hospitalisation in 2020, while recovering from the same in a locked-down city during the global pandemic, poems on the death of friends, on nightmares and insomnia. The book is the body, and you are its consciousness, perhaps negotiating the language of this writer to reach at your own individual truths. Thank you for delving into the depths of my syntax.

Nikita Parik
Kolkata
July 2022

Acknowledgements

My City is a Murder of Crows was long-listed by a British publishing house, *The Emma Press*, in their last general call for chapbook submissions. My gratitude to *The Emma Press*, and to all their editors, for long-listing my work out of 182 submissions. The same chunk was also chosen by the jury of the *Mukti Bose Memorial IPPL Young Poet Award 2022* as a winner. My warm regards and gratitude to IPPL, to the jury—Mr. Gopal Lahiri, Dr. Nabanita Sengupta, Professor Amita Ray, and Ms Anindita Bose—and to the memory of Mrs. Mukti Bose.

This Mouth is an Ocean was long-listed for the *Toto Awards for Creative Writing in English* 2022. Some of the poems from *Daylight Furrows in my Abdomen* were a part of the collection that was awarded *The Nissim Excellence in Writing Award* 2020 by TSL. The prose poems from *Vignettes of Nerve-Rush* had made it to the *Rama Mehta Writing Grant* 2021 shortlist.

Among stand-alone poems, *The Spaces We Don't Occupy* was highly commended in the *Gerard Rochford Poetry Prize* judged by Dr. Wayne Price (senior lecturer of English, University of Aberdeen), and *Stealing that Storm in a Teacup* was one of the winners in Bound India's poetry writing competition judged by Arjun Rajendran. My warm gratitude to all concerned.

Some of the poems from this collection have been read at Sahitya Akademi, Delhi, for the *Sahitya Akademi Young Writer's Meet* programme. Yet others have been used in creative writing workshops by Shamayita Sen, *A Voice of One's Own*, Kalindi College, Delhi University, and Sara Siddiqui Chansarkar, *World on a Page*, online workshop. My gratitude to Shamayita and Sara for introducing my poems to new readers in creative writing classrooms.

Some of these poems have appeared in the following online journals: Stanford University's poetry gallery (co-sponsored by the University's *Centre for Spatial and Textual Analysis* and Poetic Media Lab), *Rattle, Ucity Review, Scrawl Place, The Pangolin Review, Vayavya, Mad Swirl, Setu, Muse-Pie Press, Ekphrastic Review,* etc. My gratitude to the editors of these places.

Some of these poems have appeared in anthologies such as *Kavya Bharati*, the *Yearbook of Indian Poetry in English* 2020, the *Yearbook of Indian Poetry in English* 2021, *Poetry Conclave Yearbook* 2022, *Dreich Magazine, The Brown Critique's Home anthology, Witness: The Red River Book of Poetry of Dissent,* etc. My gratitude to the editors of these places.

My sincerest gratitude and warmest regards to Arundhathi Subramaniam ji for going through my poems and writing the blurb for it despite her busy schedule.

Thanks to Mr. Sanjeev Sethi for being a wonderful friend and mentor over the years. He has been instrumental in sharpening my poetic instincts and teaching me what measured restraint in language looks like.

I am forever grateful to my co-editors at *EKL Review* for their warm friendship, and to the

Intercultural Poetry and Performance Library for a sense of community and continuous growth. Special thanks to Dr. Amit Shankar Saha for always being so selfless with his time and energy for all literary causes and concerns.

My gratitude to my family and friends, *mere jeevan ka aadhar,* for everything. Gratitude to my publisher for trusting me and my language for a second time by soliciting this collection, and for being so perfect in their craft.

CONTENTS

My City is a Murder of Crows

Vignettes of Nerve-rush

I begin with love, hoping to end there.
—JERICHO BROWN, *The Tradition*

My City is a Murder of Crows

Scripture

My mouth is a prayer
waiting
to be translated.

It is soft light,
floating faith,
pre-dawn

lightness:
in its warmth,
a city happens.

Cityscape

(*For the conversations with the Hyderabadi Uber bike guy from Mehdipatnam to Kakatiya Hills*)

As we zoom past the city lights
etched on our Februaries,
his dialect becomes the city,

chortling at my efforts to
piece this metropolis together
in clumps of disparateness.

I had pared at its essence
with fork and knife,
tried to cut a little piece

to take back home
as a memoir.
'*Oh but you don't*

love cities like that',
he may have said.
'*They are not for possessing*'.

Glass Rotundity

That *Jhumka*-seller
near India Gate
is an eye of the sea

of people circling us,
a sea that really
is a moon, as it

waxes, then wanes,
a cyclical striptease to
entice

poets. It's a pregnancy,
as it first
swells, then contracts,

birthing and *unbirthing*
the glaze
of a hundred cities

in its wake,
and only we stray
rooted

gently swaying
on the spot
to its soft tidal rhythms.

Kalkatta

I cut my city
into a vertical slice:

a bite of metro rail,
sprinklings of steel structures
(to-be fleshed in the future),
morsels of pre-colonial
buildings;

this city, a pastiche
of scraps across eons
in this writer's pasts,
presents, and futures.

Skyscraper

When the city is not
a city, it is a strand
of your grey hair:

a shiny spike
that shines
under any light.

Jharokha

Wrapped in the fabric
of my pink *dupatta*,
Begum Bazaar is
the fabled navel in
the eye of antiquity.

The streets stomach
quaintness mutely,
like measured gulps
of *Irani* chai. We walk on,
moving in a soft-haze

of sounds and colors.
You propose a game of
make-believe. We spend
hours trying to imagine
this street a thousand

clock-years before.
I erase cable poles
and electric wires off
the canvas, then this,
then that, and then some
more. You chuckle.

We're distracted
by an *itr*-seller with old eyes
that map sadness on

old-mosque surfaces, selling
perfumes that will linger

long after it's all over.
The Charminar looks on,
as it drowns under the weight
of its own history, year after year.

Want

In your absence, this city
is a monsoon puddle:

brimful to a passer-by,
but a hollow concave

flooded with an emptiness
of which only it knows.

Chimera

(*For the hours spent with Tannistha in the premises of Makkah Masjid, Hyderabad, Telangana*)

Between *Maghrib* and *Isha* that day,
we may have sailed through
the ambiguity of linguistic living.

My consciousness— no, not my *rooh*,
but my *khudi*— may have taken flight
at the Muezzin's call. It may

or may not have flitted out
of my brown pupils, past
the borders of our bodies,

past the granite solidity around,
past chai-sellers, dream-vendors,
and high minarets in ochre and gold.

It may or may not have overseen
our covered-heads leaning
into each other, the pink of my dupatta

touching the blue of yours, before
swooping back to the ground
to where we were. Between

Maghrib and *Isha* that evening,
we may or may not have
lived an illusion.

Bangalore Talkies

A heartbreak sleeps
in your bed every night.

This October has
a borderline alcohol problem.

We trip between words
(un)written, you and I.

In my imagination, I understand
all of this too well.

In your reality, it's really the drink
that drinks you.

Survival

Post-jab, my city
is a murder of crows:

loud caws,
sharp claws,
and beaks
that may break bread,
or carry the dead.

Warmth

Thiruvanmiyur in a 360×640
topples
the edge of utterances.

Our interjections quiver
behind a cold
December screen.

Full stops and commas swim
in framed
secluded rectangles.

Silence throbs in wintertide
melting
the miles between us.

Apocalypse

Post-jab, this city
has been a stinking *Hilsa*
in a co-passenger's tote bag:

it holds promises,
but all in future tense.

Sunflowers

(After a visit to cafe Lazy Suzy, Bangalore)

The walls of this cafe are painted
yellow, and there is hot chocolate
in china snuggled in our palms.
Colors must have something to do
with memory, because the yellow
of these walls reminds me of
the yellow *Chumbak* top I'd bought
earlier today, which had cost me
more than its worth, really. Just
last week we had yellow flowers
in our hair, me and my sister,
and we had clicked a lot of pictures.
The flowers lay forgotten thereafter.
I had told you of my sunflower
obsession one autumn, shared
a picture of the painting I'd made
with so much love. We'd both agreed
on just how bad it was. The walls, yes,
the walls of this cafe are painted
yellow, and there is hot chocolate
in china snuggled in our palms.
You see the yellow of longing
in my eyes, and you say those
three words, measured and exact,

'Please Move On'.

Swimming

This evening, my city
is an old man, bent forward
in *Maghrib's Namaz*:

waves of faith
keep it afloat.

Unreal City

(*After Delhi riots, 2020*)

My niece Instagrams a snap of
her recent painting: *Unnamed,*
11"x14", Fabric Color on Canvas—
we both know the weight of a brush
on sunless days. In an alt space,
a man is lynched, a witch is burnt,
a city is tried at the stake. In her
painting, the sky is silk; roses,
talcum; ether, *pashminah.*
The city's drains are clogged
with blood, there is red on green
& saffron. You see, we have
our rituals around colors
and womanisms, me and my
niece. I hear they're live-streaming
the revolution. I want to tell her
that an image of an image
isn't the image at all. That maybe
colors won't save us anymore.
Instead, I pick up my pen,
paint this sea of sadness
in language, draw all blues
from our collective unrealities.

Unreal City: From T.S.Eliot's *The Wasteland*

Lingering

Sometimes my city
is like a poem,

pandering about
without a purpose:

a pause
impregnates its poise.

Sandwich

This morning, home
was an unexpected lilt
in a stranger's English
in an alien city:

the way he supplemented
vowels that just didn't
belong there,

between, for instance,
two consonants stuck
angrily together,

just so they'd flow out
more amicably, a hug
binding them together,
like jelly between
two dry lumps of bread.

The City Reacts to News about the War

The city is a dream drafted in stone. A night descends and jerks it into existence. Somewhere, a heel-bone cracks, letting out a scream that is at once primal and prophetic. They are now trying to slap on a plaster over a fracture that is a permanent rupture on the exoskeletal structure of this city. The site of injury has swollen to the size of a pixelated child's horror on seeing his father stay behind with a Kalashnikov. The skin is the color of gunshot screams spanning your reality and my horrified imagination. Oh but don't you know? The city is a genetic reproductive schema: it is every city to ever exist. Everything is but one thing, just as one thing swells, wiggles out, and takes the form of everything. The pavements of this city are waiting to draw life-blood from the veins of another's book-stocked windows. The cities inside our screens are waiting to know what amount of fibre-glassing will ease this intumescence.

Signification of a Sunflower

Between wakefulness
and sleep, I sometimes birth
lucid syntaxes of sunflowers

on a canvas. The petals spiral
out like repressed thoughts, a
Fibonacci of yellow thoughtlessness.

The painting of a sunflower
isn't the sunflower, of course,
but this little one has sneaked inside

my mind-crevices and made
a silent-snug home of it, like
the unremembered beginning

of dreams, or that thing that
precedes all language inside
seeds of pre-frontal cortexes.

On some days, it smells
of an absent wilderness below
blue-skied Bangalore roadways,

So I camp my canvas on the floor,
free the colours from their castles,
& paint more of these wild little things.

The City is a Synonym

for perennial beginnings. Something hits a wall,

something else crosses over, passes into another

dimension, becomes something else. Nobody

knows how to accept something as just the thing

anymore. Wilted white roses from your birthday

still exude freshness in my phone, and now

they become ink across a screen. We let nothing

really die, you see. Things end, then begin

into something else: A wilt is a waltz is *weltschmerz*.

This Mouth is an Ocean

Skyline of a Prayer

Fazr azaan breaks
the sky into two.
The lit half is a prayer.

Its glowing mouth spreads
through my language
and settles in my chest.

Maybe God is
the singular breath
that floods you whole?

Someone exhales
a muted *ardas*
somewhere.

It rises to the ether
and becomes
the sun.

All faith
prerequisites
abandonment

So this prayer
abandons me
and becomes itself.

Shapes of a Clothesline

This mouth is an Indian balcony
during the months
of *saawan* & *bhaado*: someone
tiptoes across it all day,
at the pretext of drying clothes.

Quicksilver

Your face is the sugar scrub
I apply on to my face—
a handful of grainy coarseness
that melts into my cheeks
changes form, becomes skin,
until one cannot tell
one from the other.

Confinement

The dentist injects my gums
with liquid lies. *It is for dulling
the pain,* he says. My molars
are bound in metal bands; they
slash my cheeks every time
my voice feels rebellious.
A wire is fenced over the teeth
to complete this confinement.
My tongue is confused about
any movement in this barb-wired
city; a city that looks like a bloody
war site each morning before
I brush and floss. My mouth is
Kashmir, is Palestine; is a witch,
a homosexual. My voice is waiting
to oust the fictive.

Cauchemar

This night is the mouth
of a nightmare
that spits acid on the soft flesh

of my subconscious: a gargle
of fears,
angry garrulity in alien tongues;

the fluttering veil between
a world
that is and one that isn't.

This Mouth is an Ocean

This mouth is an ocean
floating on your *tectonicity*,
its water now
swirling

between
two open jaws- a shock of skin,
tissue, raw flesh, and now

it has grown
a lingual muscle that consumes
the bone below the neck: now all teeth,
and *softnesses*, all of language too,
until

all awareness is
subsumed
underwater; all of existence is
a gasping for air.

Daydreaming on the Orthodontist's Chair

The last reality, I suppose, before this reverie
hits is the blinding dental light *sunlighting*
three doctors with metal hands who're
waiting to invade the landscape of my mouth.
I try to eclipse all fear by imagining
the yellow nuisance as an LED sunflower
in bloom, and the closest guy as
the gorgeous doctor from my favourite
American medical drama. The eyes
close and now everything is a red sea,
the sun plopped underwater, sky,
coagulated blood, stars inevitably
spinning towards black holes that are
waiting in sexual anticipation.
I am falling through a red and black
denseness: light, they say, precedes
sound, but if touch and taste enter the race,
who wins the marathon? I believe
the drilling noises were heard first,
before the slash was felt on flesh,
before hot, white pain conjured a temporary
blackout, or before blood gushed out
in ecstatic abandonment, lining the tongue
with a salty, metallic taste. Someone yells,
cement the molars, and I soar, then sense
lonely high-rises that nobody lives in
finally being erected on this mouth's edge.

Whistle-blower

This night that lives
on the other end
of your lit cigarette,
(warm & moist,
out of reach),
jerks awake
at the sound
of the watchman's
whistle.

I am lying inside
the depths
of another night,
imagining all the breath
that amplifies
this kind of shrillness:
a blow that is
a cut on the face
of blindness.

As we lay awake in our
thoughts,
our nights connive,
and decide to go to bed
to a second screech:
a train whistling
its way out of the dark.

Death by Language

[*After Katsushika Hokusai and Pablo Picasso:The Dream of the Fisherman's Wife, by Katsushika Hokusai (Japan) 1814 and Reclining Nude, by Pablo Picasso (Spain) 1932*]

Midday sun turns
muted ochre, bee-buzz
softens to a lull, I am
falling into my phone's
lock screen. As I dive
deeper, pale blue turns
azure, now sapphire,
now midnight blue;
the texture of water
is ice on gooseflesh.

Now here is the promise
of a thousand nirvanas!
Delicate pink tentacles
on skin, mouth wide-open
onto my sex, mouths that
contain thunderstorms,
mouths devoid of language,
any language, all l.a.n.g.u.a.g.e…

The sea evaporates into
sunlight- my friend laughs,
says how an orgasm is
a 'little death' in French-
"We call it la petite-mort".

Maybe all pleasure is death,
some deaths, pleasure?
His laughter echoes, then
transmorphs into Picasso
on the wall: here the woman
becomes the octopus.

I stare at it until sunlight
evaporates again, and I,
I am her, but also myself,
the octopus, & the painting
staring right back
into my own eyes.

I Catch Mother Reading Jaishankar Prasad During the Coronavirus Pandemic

Her lips mouthing *devanagari* delicately,
like a personal prayer

on the nightstand of deepest
slumber; hands holding

the book jacket like a scripture; mind
oblivious to the daughter

standing rooted across the room. A silence
starts to glow around us,

becomes a patronus keeping me
out, becomes a sphere

of light, becomes the sun: it is now
almost sacrilegious to intrude.

Daylight Furrows in my Abdomen

Separation

This morning, a kitchen
accident, and the skin
became wood, chunks
of it chipped away,
separated from the body,
dissolved into ash, not
quite unlike this heart
in some kinds of absences.

Zuw Myon

You gifted me a sorrow and forgot your gift
I remain so obliged, it weighs me down
                    – Faiz Ahmed Faiz
                    (tr. Keki N. Daruwalla)

I bottled that sorrow in a pretty glass jar,
see?
Sealed the golden lid shut with mellow
paraffin.
Labeled it *Zuw Myon*, and hid it under my
skin.
I carried its dull ache around for many a year,
until
one day its throbbing refused to give in.

So I retrieved it from under my
epidermis,
fed it wood smoke, bathed it in full-
moon magick,
carried it around like sun-kissed
bliss.

And this time, it accompanied
me like

a glowing talisman, a warm patronus,
so I
broke open the lid one night. Through

the sharp-
edged light I saw letters blossoming
like
fireflies, nouns clenching and declench-
ing inside
Mexican daisies, sharp yellow and
white.

And I knew just what needed to be
done.
I swallowed it whole, and a new
tongue
glided over the ghost of my last
one.

Zuw Myon is a Kashmiri phrase of adoration

Affliction

One summer, I inhaled
your absence with the breeze.
It has infested my lungs.
Its wet heaviness has since
lingered, cohabiting, coexisting,
as if in a symbiotic relationship.
Some nights, it becomes
the *giloy* creeper that had died
under my watch and never
bore leaves. On said nights,
it climbs my throat, chokes
my breath, silently strangles
my ability for language.
On other days, I sneeze some
of it out onto paper. Call it poetry.
To transcend grief, you must
allow it to fill you. How do you
transcend absences?

Stealing that Storm in a Teacup

To fall in love is to create a religion that has a fallible God

– Borges

That year when summer
butterflied into
winter, I *caterpillared*
into a thief. Your dialect
was the first to go;
its lilts transitioned
into a guitar riff, which I
sneakily secured
inside my bones.

Your mind's morphology
I morphed into a semblance
of sanity across my skies.
That lone cigarette we'd
once shared became
the sun inside dark
alleys of my eyes.

Your shifting identities
I stole over time,
cataloguing them into
neat rows for
perusal in lonelier times.

I stole and stole until I

became a salient
museum of your *youness*.
Now this museum is
just another brick
and mortar in a city
learning to steal differently.

Note: *Storm In A Teacup* is a song by Red Hot Chilli Peppers.

Malaise

This morning
is your left eyebrow: look

how it rises,
now falls,
now rises again.

Daylight furrows
in my abdomen,

a knit,
an arch,
a dreamy collapse.

Creation

This existence is
a cave
caged in unknowing.

My consciousness
and yours— two
primitives

figuring out
the aesthetics
of *everythingness*.

You rub
your words
against mine,

A fire
is borne
out of stone.

Circles

On a page
a word
stirs.

Stirring stalks
flower
buds of May.

May showers
tease
our forlorn skies,

Skies that mate,
then split
to birth a language:

this language that is
shaped like
a yellow flower.

A yellow flower
crowns
my pretty heartache,

a heartache that weaves
sunsets
around a single word:

a single word
that stirs
on my lonely page.

Timothy Green (Editor, *Rattle*) comments:

A note included with the submission explained that this form is called *AnthAdi*, a style long-used in Tamizh literature, in which the variation of the ending word of the first stanza becomes the first word of the next stanza. I'd never heard of this form before, and I love the way the short lines move gracefully down the page—it sings with quiet introspection. But what made me keep coming back was the mystery of what the 'single word' might be. Especially when combined with the visual art, Nikita's poem manages to tell a whole story without ever telling the story.

Drag

(*After T.S.Eliot's* The Preludes)

Tonight *the burnt-out*
ends
of smoky days

singe unsuspecting
paws of
stray emotions

as they entice vagrant
drag-desires
into indignity,

polluting our meaning
-less
geographies.

Tonight, they litter sidewalks
and streets
like entry-level poetry.

Shards

(After Fragments sculpted by Bruno Catalano)

The shreds of soul
you left behind
when a new city
consumed you
float in my ether
like dream-catchers.

Opaque
dragonfly-wing bodies
glittering in the sun,
thousands of them—

rising after sundown
like an army
of delusional fanoosh
visible from tiny
train windows
of a city lost in time.

What fills the chunks
of your hollowed soul?
What becomes of these
ripped excerpted *yous*?

Self-betrayal

Girl in love
is a ripe alphonso

allowing knifes
to cut through

her soft core: flesh
friends with blade.

Vignettes of Nerve-Rush

01. 01. 22

Sun's full rotation:
an entire year of chasing
its shadows indoors.

Year of the Plague

This aurora, once rosa
multiflora, now sleeps
in morbid orchids, dead
foraminifera. I trace

your face in florid hues,
in *Neelkamal's* blues,
in the drops of dew on
wilted *Gudhals*. The nights

are aquiver, much like
that black river from one
town of sinners I escaped
from. Its drones, its
silent phones, are

dulcet tones of a death-trance.
But the flowers!
The flowers, they tell,
that a sanguine scull
will beat this lull,

and this aurora,
now dead foraminifera,
will once again be
rosa multiflora.

Alchemy

(*For an unexpected friend*)

For you, after daylight curdled, all blood turned to coffee. Now every time the mind tries to get some sleep, it kicks up a storm and jerks you awake. The thoughts remain perpetually dunked in the last dregs of blackness, refusing milk, or sugar, or a view outside of the coffee mug. I want to take a sieve and filter out all the sticky darkness, extract just the right amount of white light to split into a lightness that is the shape of dreamless slumber. Each night, we lift time in our palms and pacify it to take more space inside of your sleep-cocoon. Each night, we try to alchemize the coffee back to blood.

The Spaces We Don't Occupy

(*For Hemant, gone too soon*)

One minute, you are a boy on the
edge
of quivering possibilities, the next

a speck of white light, a tear on
the face
of your mother, and all mothers

who have silently hovered around
you, quiet
maternal fortitude, warm cicadas,

in moving spheres, you know, like
mothers usually are.
I think of you, and the sheer vastness

you now embody, and would someone
please
tell me what becomes of spaces

that *were*, that *used to be*, and now
just aren't:
trapped air between hands enveloping

a brother in a hug, the chasm between
a handshake,
places that collect drops of sweat,

and vacuums that are pushed away
by moist, warm
breath? What becomes of it all?

Flow

(*For Iram Shaikh*)

You speak in tongues of fire: syllables rushing out wildly as if escaping incendiary explosions. Yesterday, the left foot buckled and a warm pain shot up from the calves and into the glutes: a neural network consumed by fire in the forest of the body. The red from the flames rose up, reached the skyline of your eyes, burnt down the shy walls between internal and external to the embers. Look at all that black smoke swirling underneath the pupils, swirling time and reality in its swift cyclical dance. I marvelled at how the gushing syllables still flowed on, unaffected, as you continued to speak of this and that. Are *aag* and *aab* that far off if you ignore the end consonant in one tipsy moment of sugar high? If you could just sneakily replace one bilabial sound with a guttural sound, look how quickly water turns to fire.

Improv

(*CMRI Hospital, August 2020*)

This fever is a black garden ant that rises then falls then rises then falls then rises then falls; me, its iris, watching it rising and falling from dawn through dusk, following its trail from lonely afternoon rains to the cold of pre-dawns. This cold isn't environmental, this cold is inside me. This cold is me- clattering teeth dancing to the orchestra of fear, sweat pouring from skin onto skin, a cold clawed deep inside the chest. I design the death of my days.

A hard slap of a swab inside the nose, then throat. Once, then twice. The foreignness of big, bright rooms with beeping machines and blue-robed strangers who come and go in diastolic rhythms. A green vein becomes the divided highway between illness and anti-illness. A needle punctuates it, then fills it with more foreignness. Something passes through it and reaches the heart, this little lump of life that's been beating uncontrollably, almost in a rebellion. It runs, afraid, into stray nerves, into the isolated pit of my *arpeggioed* stomach, then back up into the throat. Who said rebels don't experience fear? It shocks and stuns with its erratic beats, the pastiche of an experimental drumming sequence in an alt-rock song.

Outside the window
a city awakens into consciousness,
a forgotten riff

Static

(*CMRI Hospital, August 2020*)

Now is the cold, grounding presence of a thermometer under the tongue, gently pressing its metallic aloofness against delicate flesh. Like a lover, the thermometer gifts you awareness. All *thens* have become a non-entity as time thieves around the body of my isolated space, snatching away feverish hours from the threads of memory. I try to recount passing days with the number of thermometer jabs: on a good day, 3 for 1.
There is a formlessness to the shadowy physicality of existence oscillating between illness and uncertainty. It obstinately stares into the eyes of my collective lived experiences, clicking its pincers in anxiousness. *Did we love enough, live enough, do enough?* I am tired but this mass of body, strangely my own, won't let me sleep. The 'I' is an intruder in this physical reality: this 'I' that questions and prays, reasons and *unreasons*, doubts and loves.

Urgent Prayers
rushing into night's mouth,
an *eternalness*

Amp

(CMRI Hospital, August 2020)

The nurse turns off the lights unceremoniously at 2 am. A luminous darkness shivers with an unprecedented tiredness. Something lives under the periphery of this eyelid. It craves mother's touch and father's gentle caresses. It chokes on fear and decides to crawl out from under my shut eyelid to traverse the externality in the dark: the inviting vastness of the warm epidermis. There is dry, crusted blood on the left wrist, a spatial rupture in an otherwise whole point in time. The drip is almost empty by now, its pressure weakening. The blue liquid inside the bottle of sanitizer blinks under the discontinuous city lights. A shuffle of feet outside the door to the left. What sleeps and what is awake? What moves in the realm of the unconscious, and what examines this sober reality?

Crippling Fear,
a ten-headed monster:
we feed off each other

The Night's Eye

is a throbbing vein
inside of a girl

who tries to decipher
the method to
your madness, Sylvia.

She paints inverted
moons, dashes & virgules,
soft cocoons

of your will to
confess. She picks
a rock, a wonder of

stars, a choice of
camouflage,
magicks them all

with ink of her scars,
and there emerge
vignettes of nerve-rush

dressed as paroxysm
of the bedlamed
babble of being.

The rough magick's
begun, Sylvia.
Can't you trace,

among the socketed
white stars,
your face?

Note: *among the socketed white stars, your face—* line from a Sylvia Plath poem

Drone

(Post-hospitalisation, October 2020)

This city is an uncertainty experiencing itself in a blur of light and sound. It eyes me hungrily while an October engulfs its plague-ridden ribs. A damselfly perches itself on its nose, its opaque wings reflecting the city's entirety in a riot of colours: bright, bright sunshine is seen dulling the ambulance lights bouncing past its many lanes. A feather is twirling gracefully in the air somewhere as your anxiety gets ready to position itself outside an ICU wall elsewhere. A collective sigh is now precipitating from the brow of the day, its sticky wetness persistent like adamant Calcutta sweat. Someone sustains a dull chord over and over and over again to the effect of waking sleepiness.

orange sunshine
eats all light:
a guitar drones on

Now too many things happen all at once: an evening descends, a charm breaks, the damselfly takes off, taking with itself the comfort of a pain that is reflected, impersonal, distanced... unreal?

A Ghazal for the Art of Free-falling

A blue serenity has forested where a stillness blooms,
A cold fire now abounds where a stillness blooms

I shut my eyes, a calmness sweeps me over
Silence like a song sounds where a stillness blooms

Existence is but one deep breath centred into self,
Purposeful breathing resounds where a stillness blooms

This life is a droplet hanging on the eyelash of fate,
Forgiveness is profound where a stillness blooms.

Drown yourself in this river, Nikita, for
Being lost is being found where a stillness blooms

Vibrato

(For Rahul; Post-hospitalisation, October 2020)

Now is the envy of all of the dead, you say. Now is the envy of all of the dead, I chant. Around me, thoughts and things garland to form infinite realities. The Giloy sprouts new leaves, one squirrel eats up the old ones, that ginger cat chases the squirrel across the Neem's 200-year old bark. A *presentness* vibrates in me so hard that everything in the vicinity gets strummed at the exact same note.

a spot in time:
nowness,
the only reality

Now is the envy of all of the Dead—Don Hertzfeldt (*World of Tomorrow*).

Memory in Acrophobia

(*Notes from mid-air, Bir, Himachal Pradesh*)

The world at fifteen-hundred-
-plus feet above
sea level is

the shivering underbelly
of a birdling thrown
roughly into air.

At this height, dangling midair,
with the sun poking
at the pupils,

body freezing up
in revolt, something gross
rising in the esophagus,

and comfort of land
many unrealistic airkicks away,
physics changes.

Air becomes water, its waves
pulling at your atoms
in all directions; sky

turns into gravity, sucking
you away from home.
Home is an incomprehensible

dot in a maze of green;
and you, you're a frozen brain,
cold clay body,

nerves of rust,
fervently praying
for a miracle.

Eye of a Ripple

The act of remembrance is a rusty apparatus at fall filled with water from summers gone by. A ripple forms: it is now the past, and in a minute, we are going to listen to Mozart in a taxi that's floating on the streets of New Delhi. The sounds are barely out of your phone's speaker when the city erupts all around us like some *fireworked* sea on ecstasy. The waves spill and surge, and now there is a crescent bite of a crescendo in your hair, fragments of Delhi chill nestled in our collarbones, nuggets of sound chips scattered across our laps like fallen frangipanis. An ebb, a flow, we are dripping in phonic *saltsprays*.

The ripple flattens
Sounds wane:
Sun shearing water

Sound of a Scream

(After super-cyclone Amphan, Kolkata 2020)

This night splinters the throat
of a scream, then chokes it
into unbecoming. It drowns
in the cyclonic winds, a mask
covering its muted mouth.

This scream tries to navigate
its way through a darkness
that's tar; black, black tar coating
city-walls with electricity-less pasts.

This water that's rising
in the streets prods this scream
for a memory it doesn't possess.
It wants to run away. Only,
there's no place to go.

It tumbles on the sloping
wet surface of my house—
broken glass, uprooted trees
sharp metals,

and teaches the world that there's
more blood than sound
to some kinds of screams.

Reverb

(*Post-hospitalisation, 2020*)

An illness has taken hostage of this body and upturned the hourglass of my being. Somebody else lives in this consciousness now, this somebody who has singed my relish for the soft coldness of dusks, dark rooms, and all things wet and icy. Instead, I now find in me a perpetual seeking for the sun.

Like a lover, I observe the changing texture of its rays through the day—soft muslin during early hours, Sikkimese wool at noon, pinafored and layered cotton before dusk. It filters through the many layers of my curls and makes love to my face in strange geometric shapes. Like a needle, it then ruptures my skin and enters this body. Doesn't leave. Lingers all night like certain thoughts.

sun's spread
on my skin:
dada's warm shawl

Hiraeth

My grandfather's ancestral house

is a smirk

on the face of

urban connectivity.

It is cool water

from mud-pitchers

during desert summers,

a rhododendron

at dawn, liquid gold

when the sun sets.

My grandfather's ancestral house

used to have turbaned men

speaking in tongues

of earthy *bajra* and *chaas*,

a community-well

where women sang

in colors of *gangaur*,

a little courtyard

where little children

played *pitthu* all summer.

My grandfather's ancestral house

is now a hairline fracture

in the ankle

of modernity:

stone and rubble,

plants growing through

cement, stench

of abandonment. It is

comatosed hours, poetry in paralysis,

a calendar of absences.

Tremolo

(*Post-hospitalisation, 2020*)

I walk from room to room all night in the effort to tire myself into sleeping. The house opens its many eyelids and watches me glide in the darkness. I am the ghost it sometimes imagines. I am not real, it convinces itself, because how can I possibly be? There are red veins in the whiteness around its pupils. It is a deserted museum trained in hopeless *waitings*. Right about now, it is watching and *unwatching* reality unfolding itself in the shape of a girl dressed in its translucent nightmares. But indeed, this is all a dream—the girl, the walking, the clocked footsteps that sound like the systole and diastole of these walls?

Time's treachery
a breathing corpse
the eye of an I

Anatomy of In-Betweening

This window is an idea
swimming in crosscurrents
of being and unbeing.
It falters

like a broken
compass needle,
a desperate dance
of dazed delusions.

A bit of sky is
roughly stitched
over its loose epidermis:
the hospital gown

of a corpse still warm
in the newness of death.
There's some life
in the act of dying too,

but what becomes
of a thought that needs
anesthesia to be?

1s and 0s

This body is an automatic that drops on the nearest solid surface and powers off the eyes in this lesser reality. In a hyper-reality, it is googling *Five Tips to Remain Productive in an Apocalypse.* Even when the eyes close in one plane of existence, they remain wide, wide awake in all others. The parts of me that live inside screens have now broken themselves free of me to become something I barely recognise. I am now dreaming of the apps that become me in my nightmares: I'm the cyclical movement of eyes across a screen as it scrolls by itself over absurd wish-lists; now I am a voice in my head and letters across boxed textual frames. I am not solid anymore: I am a mere phantom itch for my corporeal existence. First, the sound of a tsunami overpowers everything, and next, I am drowning, drowning, drowning in a wave of 1s and 0s, symbols and logos, until a claustrophobia jerks me awake.

Sliced silence
of the night:
eye-sockets across a floor.

Remember, remember, this is now, and now, and now. Live it, feel it, cling to it. I want to become acutely aware of all I've taken for granted.

SYLVIA PLATH

PRAISE FOR NIKITA PARIK

"Her writing is a revelation of lightness and agility. That she manages to keep her facility for language during a period where it often disappears is a miracle. With elegant wordplay, rolling energy and intense sensitivity, this collection tracks the path of nostalgia and cultural footprint, dream and desire."

Gopal Lahiri, THE STATESMAN

"The source of such deftness is Parik's academic training. She has studied French and English and Linguistics. This is her debut collection, but it has the confidence of a poet sure of her craft."

Uttaran Das Gupta, BUSINESS STANDARD

"Nikita Parik's debut collection *Diacritics of Desire* experiments with different stanza forms, with thoughts coupled with terms from linguistics in an organic way to create an interesting tonal sweep: the "cedille" in French "eliminates/ the rough [K]s in the French language"; "why is the c in 'coeur' still harsh/ in this tongue,/ if not by the design of desire?". Parik acculturates the English language with localisms: Jugni, papad, mangori, Padharo Mahare Des, jogan and rangrez make the English lines jingle vibrantly."

THE JOURNAL OF COMMONWEALTH LITERATURE 2020

"Nikita invents a new class of language with her almost arithmetic cellular pods– plastic, cellophane, uniquely solid and compact with a transparent gauze. The title of the first poem 'Phonetic Maze' is rather apt for what follows, burrows and lanes of longing woven into syllables and dialects, lisp and vowels, a stretched stutter and poised control."

Aakriti Kuntal, Setu

"Nikita Parik writes poems as if she is drowning but without dying because there is a constant instinctive struggle to resurface. The air in her lungs is all she has and she does not have a choice but to create bubbles to survive. What fills the bubbles is no longer a part of her. It no longer remains her language but becomes the language of her poems. Nikita's poems are a language in itself because they speak to the readers in that universal cognitive sense."

Amit Shankar Saha, Bengaluru Review

"Parik writes in a very impressionistic way, playing with language and ideas. I felt invited into her explorations. In the poem "Phonetic Maze," Parik hints at the elusiveness of reality. How words act like "lithe talismans" connecting aspects of our identities."

Mike Fiorito, Mad Swirl